Citycarrier

"Compassion is the chief law of

human existence"

Fyodor Dostoyevsky

The Idiot

Citycarrier

Stories from the Street

Rob Wilson

SETTLED REST PUBLISHING

Dedicated to Letter Carriers

"All these rely on their hands,

and all are skillful in their own work.

Without them no city can be inhabited . . .

They do not sit in the judge's seat . . .

But they maintain the fabric of the world,

and their prayer is in

the exercise of their trade"

Sirach (Ecclesiasticus) 38:31-34

"Poetry I take to be

the continual effort

to bring language back

to the actual"

C. S. Lewis

Letters

Preface

What follows are stories (true only insofar as I remember them!), character sketches, and impressions gathered while walking the time-worn streets of a Montana City Letter Carrier route, some eight miles daily, from 2012 to 2016.

Names and some details have been altered to protect privacy.

Postal delivery has always been about connecting humanity. I am grateful to have been connected in turn with all the people the reader may glimpse in these pages. Sharing in their lives has deepened my own.

Rob Wilson   April, 2018

"Stories bind us by reminding us

that our lives all exhibit the same fragilities,

and thus demand

that we stay humane"

William Kittredge

A Hole in the Sky

Table of Contents

Citycarrier

Stories from the Street

Re-membered

Squeezing between old brick apartment
        blocks,
I duck under pinned rows of frozen
        laundry
Hung out in the cold screaming wind:
Untimely shorts and threadbare t-shirts
Starched in grey clumps by ice.

Like monochrome prayer flags
They clumsily flap their corporate logos,
Pleading simply,
"Remember me."

Open Stops

Stripedsnake plays me like a flute
This morning for his check,
Smoothly,
No harder than breathing,
Fingers fluttering over holes in my shell.

Used to hearing No,
He rides up on a bike later,
A different approach,
So soft, so still
He almost takes me in.

I tell him I wish I could
Ignore the Man's instructions,
Break the rote.
He gauges me and leaves again.

He knows by now when I'll be where.
Used to waiting,
He hangs around town,
That urgent trip he pleaded
Forgotten.

He knows all my stops.

And then at four he passes by again
On yet another sidewalk.
Without pausing he plainly calls out,
"Thanks, mailman!"
Without a trace of irony.

My deliveries made,
Our parts played,
It is him I cannot gauge.

Sub-zero Hero

The beard I did not grow this fall
Weighs heavier with each puffing step
Up the ice-clogged stairs.

Every breath becomes knit
Into the balaclava's
Government Issue acrylic,
Cleaving to my chin and upper lip.

At zero my glasses fogged up
Meeting the merciful blast
Of a radiator-gorged apartment lobby,
Then glazed in wavy ice layers outdoors
To adjust my refraction twice.

At ten below snot freely flows,
Freezing into faux pearl buttons
On my blue nylon jacket
Ragg-mittened hands can't wipe away.

Unlike my cell phone,
The Thermos flask of coffee
Is not yet frozen,
But the screw-on cup handle
Snaps cleanly off,
Brittle in my throbbing grip.

O all that the mail
Must go through!

Unseen

How many times
Did I knock at his entry,
The basement apartment,
Waiting impatiently
For him to open.

Loud shuffling,
Objects clunking within,
"Hold yer horses! I'm coming!"
He'd holler breathlessly,
Finally throwing open the heavy door,
Extending his hands to me
And cocking his head.

I expected to smell alcohol,
Until I realized it was urine.

How many times
Did he awkwardly pause
And squint
And linger too long
Before shutting.

Perhaps he was wondering
How I'd failed to see
That the weekly package read
"FREE MATTER FOR THE BLIND."

Pealing

When the Cathedral bell rings
Around noon each weekday,
Students at the school next block
Know soon their class will end.
Idlers on the street are moved
To wonder where their lunch may be.
Lawyers lock their office doors
And keep the Courthouse clock count.

Just a handful of souls
Migrate to the Source
Of all this pealing:
An intimate meal,
A wafer and a sip of wine.

Quietly
Spirit and matter meld,
Mysterious alchemy
Just down the road.
Raise your eyes to see Nothing,
Leave fed for eternity
In two gulps.

For whom then does the bell toll?

Compound Eyes

The mud wasps have taken up
        dwellings
Directly across from one another,
One in the middle of each half
Of the numeral 8
Appended in three dimensions
To the clapboard siding
Of this house.

They shift toward me
Like cockeyed pupils
Crossing as I walk the porch
To stuff letters
In the mailbox
Beside the numbers
Of the house,
Their home,
On eighth street.

Mansion Tour

May I be ennobled
By these works
Through which I walk daily.

Firmly founded
On quarried stone,
Chiseled to turn out
A pillar.

Truly crafted—
Not mere device.
Lit graciously
Within and without.

Judiciously proportioned,
Yielding delight
By various parts.

Like this inviting portico
Open to take in
And to return.

Grandfathered

Here at this park point
Behind the library
You found me that day
Loading my bag.

You drove up holding a latte
For your decaf bride
Just back at the midwife's
Down the street.

With wonder and relief
You told me of your daughter born
Not two hours since.

So I am Grampa yet again.
This time right here,
Standing over the storm drain
To which I've come from so far
To be grounded.

I lock up the truck,
Walk into six law offices
To exchange the morning post,
Wearing tear-brimming eyes
And a shameless grin.

Wild Life

As the woman bends down
To sign for the letter I hold,
I glance warily past
Her tattooed neck
Toward the barking dog behind her.

Avoiding eye contact,
I look left instead,
And am face to face
With a brilliant green parrot
Perched on her shoulder.

He makes no comment,
Cocking his garish head
To better size me up
With his unfathomable eye.

Election Year

Incongruously,
There's a US Senator
On the steps of the Craftsman:
The unmistakable bulk of
Big Jon Flattop, the farmer.
With his top shirt button undone
Beneath the straining sport coat,
He shifts uncomfortably
While the camera crew fiddles
Four paces back.

Seizing my opening,
I swing through the white picket gate
Toward the porch mailbox,
Nodding, "Hey, Jon,"
As I rush by.

He catches my eye—
A master of contact—
And thanks me.
For what?
My work?
The distraction?
My vote?

Surely even he can't recall
That I've been his correspondent.

In the backyard the ankle-biter barks
        at me,
(I suppose Jon has already won him
        over)
And across the avenue a voice yells out,
"I guess you lied, Jon!"

There's got to be a simpler way
For a guy to make a living.

Walkup

She came home
From the hospital
A foot short.

Black crepe wrapping
The stump,
She stilted
Up the wood staircase
Toward the smell of frybread.

Her old man fumbles
To open the door for her,
More awkward than
Her phantom gait.
She shouts him off.

The steps of the walkup
Loom ahead
Now and each day
Of her shortening life.

Grace

I moved right
To the sidewalk's edge,
Making way for a chattering couple
Coming toward me
This late summer evening.

The woman bundled something
In her arms—a baby?
No, a bouquet,
From which she handed me
A single white carnation,
As she smiled,
Nearly singing out,
"Something that smells good
For you to carry!"

We all three laughed.
Shared delight
Graced my sweaty satchel strap
A couple more blocks
Before falling out somewhere.

The aroma of kindness
Lingered longer.

Diamond Brady

In the basement apartment
Off the back alley
Beside the laundry room,
He liberates light
From dirty baubles.

Skillfully he pares away
Accretions
Down to true color,
Shaving towards brilliance.

Brady himself, though,
Always sports grey stubble,
Wears solid dark colors.
Steely blue-eyed,
Vise-jawed,
He only sparkles
When he shows off
The delicate art
Of his tremulous hands.

Shaking a gemstone from
An old registered envelope,
He holds it up to the sun for me:
Thirty thousand, he says:
Beautiful!

Drawing it out
Was a good day's work.
He flips and pockets it,
Shambles off to the Jeweler,
And then to the bar
Before it closes.

Round About Epiphany

Saturday morning,
So cold there's no one out
As I drive past the park
In bright sub-freezing sun.

But when I emerge
From the condo tower
Across the street,
A lone figure skater
Is twirling on the frozen duck pond,
All flash and grace in a skirt and a scarf
To dazzle the small gaggle
Of displaced geese

And the slack-jawed mailman
In his four layers of wool,
Breathless.

Longrunner

He could charm the skin off a snake
While he stroked it in his hands.

He made me enjoy the ritual
Of dragging out his VA meds
From the stacks in my van
Just a few minutes ahead,
If I would.
Oh, and he'd take his check too,
If I didn't mind;
Might as well
While I'm at it!
(Come in handy, I guess)

He was on his way out of town, you see.
Not to the rez this time,
But for a weekend fishing trip.
I asked what they catch there,
Just to hear him talk.
"Oh . . . fish," he affirmed.

Dropping a different line,
He plumbed me,
"You a vet too? Thought so."
(Good odds around here)

The next week he made the front page,
Drowned in the Missouri
Swimming to an island
At one a.m. to join the party.
The current caught up with him.

His niece I'd never seen before
Adorned the papers grieving.
The woman whose home he shared
Preferred not to play the bereft widow.
Was she tired of smooth talk?
Was he caught in a lie?
Or did she simply envy
The ease of his escape?

Lower North Side

My boss mumbles that the dammed
     river
Gathers its flotsam and jetsam here.

In low-crouching office blocks
Behind blinded Justice's back,
Hungry lawyers dust their books
And wait.

In a warren of puzzle-cut old homes
Stoic Indians linger,
Named only when their checks arrive.

Fine old mansions intervene,
Stuffed with catalogs
And prominent citizens,
Who, with easy western grace
Do clear their walkways
And even curb their dogs.

Cheek to jowl in dense brick blocks
A transient cast of characters
Warms concrete apartment steps
With cigarette butts,
Politely holding open the lobby door
For another dubious couch coming off
An equally battered pickup truck
Towing a Montana moving van:
A livestock trailer.

Stone churches toll bells,
The brick school circulates young
            humanity
Like a pumping heart,
And Canada geese do own the park,
Despite what people wish.

And the former Convent
Yet testifies to a Higher Power
(Plus eleven other steps)
With the grace of Strong Coffee,
As it weekly graduates
The sober once again.

Duty in Drama

Two men stood out on the asphalt
Of the side street I was crossing.
They conversed in hushed tones
Facing a townhouse door.
But one wore a bulky black vest,
And their cars parked together
Were conspicuously unremarkable.

Still I was seized cold
As I reached up to the stairtop mailbox
At that apartment's door,
And a young blond woman
Burst out of it and yelled
Around me across the street.
Her sobs obscured her words
Even as they traced her anguish.
She withdrew slamming the door.

"What did she say?"
Asked one man,
Voicing my own question.

I raised my eyes from descending
          the broken-up steps
To see which man had spoken,
And noticed the handcuffs
Binding the unvested one.

A uniformed cop,
Newly arrived,
Grasped this man's shoulder
Almost tenderly,
Leading him without words
To the back seat
Of a decaled cruiser,

While I climbed the next steps
Of each subsequent townhouse,
Remembering to breathe,
And wondering . . .
Praying.

BFF?

Knots of younger girls
Trailing from the grade school
Braid light and dark together
As they weave along the sidewalks
      home,
Boldly teasing out who said what
      to who
(And, mostly, why),
Flashing easy smiles.

But time will come
When they are brushed apart,
Separated for color,
Angst replacing giggles.

They will grow quieter,
With keenly focused eyes
Absorbing cues
While emitting
Next to nothing.

Covert

Behind the door mail slots,
Double dozens of dogs
Whimper, bark and slather
At my footfall on their porches.

Just two, though, growl softly,
Meeting the inserted bundle
With ravenous jaws
That snap up the mail
And fling it broken-necked
Upon the floor inside.
They are victors every day
In a game that never grows old.

But it is at one of the other doors
That a flyer catches in the slot flap.
So I bend down to look,
To retrieve it without tearing it,
And I expose the slightly cocked eyes
Of a different player within:
Dilated feline pupils
Locking onto mine
Noiselessly.

Urgent Care

A young airman with a whitewall
        haircut
Stands in gym shorts in January,
Stomping his feet on the Rectory porch
As he pleads out ice fog
        like a censer
To the hard-of-hearing secretary
For Father to hear his confession.

But it's not Tuesday today.

I cross the street away from his voice
But watch him gesticulate,
Flinging his hands
As if to shake off something caustic,
Something he's done.

I wonder that in one man,
Without self-consciousness,
Unclean hands
And a heart that would be pure
Might coexist.

Resident Alien

Walter the Fed Chief
Thanks <u>you</u> for asking,
Slipping in a catch breath
And pushing up the bridge of his
      glasses
Before expounding on another opinion,
Full voice,
To overcome the loud arterial traffic
Just ten feet away
From his shotgun apartment door.

Yeah, he is from New Jersey,
But he knows where every fire in
      Montana is burning,
As well as he knows today's
      equity markets,
As well as he knows the proper way
      to make really good matzo—
Information he dispenses freely,
But only when asked.

"I wondered why you'd been
      putting mail in that box;
It hasn't been used in years!"

And, most truly,
"Slow down!
They'll just give you more work
        if you hurry!"

Listen:
I can take good advice.
When they trim my route down
        below a thousand stops,
Walter's block goes to another carrier.

One morning in the break room
        newspaper
I read his small-print free death notice,
And say,
I won't forget him.

The Luxe

A stocky young man,
Goateed,
In jeans and a black metal t-shirt,
Stealthily wheels used tires
Through the mosaic tile lobby
Over the basement ballroom
Into the decrepit brass cage elevator

Up to his whispering, waiting wife,
Two at a time,
Like Noah slouching toward
        apocalypse,
Carefully evading the Manager.

Barber Shop

The barber pole is static painted wood,
Timeless as the shotgun flat roof home
And shop to which it is secured,
"The oldest Barber Shop in town--
     56 years,"
The eighty-something barber assures me
     grinning.

Though rattled from his nap
Beneath the newsprint coverlet
As I let slam the screen door,
He rallies nicely now.

His wife's quiet smile welcomes me too
As she exits the adjacent chair
Into the house to make lunch.
I roll the dice and drop into its warmth.
A rubber apron sails over me,
And I am caught like a fly in a web.

The contract is sealed by his pointing
To the penciled wall sign:
HAIRCUT $16.
I nod for the last time in 40 minutes.

After the clipper's raucous chatter,
Large shocks of grey hair fall silently
Beneath his slightly shaking scissors.

At last is unsheathed
A formidable straight razor.
Seeing him ply the strop,
I recall Boot Camp,
And he warms to the topic
Of lather and whitewalls.
I revert to habits of submission
With sharp steel poised tremulously
      at my neck,
Until he commandeers the soapbox.

His stories seem fable and fact alloyed:
Mining silver and copper and coal;
Strikes, threats, hold-ups, near misses.
"Always be careful;
Watch yourself.
Trim your nose hairs?
Shall I do your eyebrows?"

Had I raised them?

I opt out, pleading lunch break is over:
Better go or I'll be delivering
        in the dark.
Oh, no, he concedes,
This neighborhood's no place to be
        at night,
Telling how he kicked the knife away
From the thug in the alley.
A stiff bristle brushing
And firm-fingered anointing
Of vintage pomade
Punctuate his point nicely.

As we settle up (NO CHECKS!)
He balks at my accounting:
"Too many singles."
They're for you, I insist,
Just pleased to leave whole:
The most careful haircut I ever got.

We exchange handshakes,
Both satisfied we've played our roles
        right.
The next day I breathe easier
When I see his chair filled
With another customer.

Comment Withheld

No, I won't walk past your dog.
I'm sure she's fine,
But she's not mine,
And she doesn't want me here.

No, I will not pet your dog.
I'm sure he's sweet,
But he eats meat;
Don't say he doesn't bite.

PinkMan

He wears his loss all over,
From shoes to shorts to watch cap,
Throbbing pink like a hammered thumb
Plump and shining.

Devoid of hair and guile and tact,
He speaks freely but precisely,
Questioning me to be sure
I haven't opened his copy of Playboy.

He bikes down the sidewalk,
Wrapped in a pink hoody,
Dangling white plastic grocery bags:
Marshmallows in cotton candy cloud.

I love him for his fierce loyalty,
Not to some pampered Celebrity
Or to any pandered Brand,
But to his lost Love unnamed.

He is no blueblood,
Nor is he ragged red and sore.
He just bleeds pink—
And makes onlookers wince.

Drugstore Indian

To stay a step ahead of the next eviction,
He gets his mail forwarded
To three nearby porch-front mailboxes
      of working neighbors
He monitors discreetly.

The beat cop tracked me down
Behind the Post Office counters
To ask if I knew where he lived.
I only know where he no longer lives.

Then one day he missed a pickup.
The neighbor told me there must be
      some mistake,
And would I send this package back?
Yes, I'll get it to him.

She may be a nurse,
But she didn't know it was insulin;
And I hate to see him crash,
Even if the judge does say
He can't live here anymore.

Fair Play

Tanner the Rehab Dog is becoming.

Not that there's anything beautiful
In her furtive German Shepherd creep
          and graying muzzle,
Nor is she training for credentials
          as a therapy dog.
Like others here she is a work
          in progress.

Sometimes she's just a piece of work.
Like when she's off leash outdoors
          with staff on smoke break,
And shoots off after a passing mutt
          bound to its terrified walker.

Tanner's nose is stuck inseparably
          to the back of my satchel
Whenever I bring in the mail,
Closer to my pepper spray
Than is my own hand.
I baby-talk her,
Calling her by name.
She growls softly.

But she met her match
When Tabs the Detox Cat showed up,
Leaping deftly on to the admission desk
To claim higher ground.

Tanner yelped and ran down the hall
Followed gamely by Tabs.

Turnabout happens.

High Jumper

Having heard the sirens keening
An hour and five blocks ago,
I take it in stride
When the yellow police tape
Encircling dried blood and glass shards
Forces me off the sidewalk.

Around both wings of the four-story
        apartment block,
Past the locked back door,
I carry mail for 59 boxes
I'm determined to unload.
The lobby bench regulars will be
        waiting by now.

For once the maintenance man is
        tight-lipped,
Mumbling only about a "high jumper."
The TV news cameraman packs his gear
A flight upstairs to his apartment,
Home:
Local coverage.

His colleague,
The intern weather girl,
Will skip tonight's late shift.
She had left her neighboring door ajar
For her girlfriend,
Her producer,
Across the hall,
When a strange young man sped
In and out instead
Straight to and through
Her third-floor window.

Over the flower beds
And strip of lawn
To the sidewalk
His mad momentum took him.

He was dead before the aid car came
          a dozen blocks.
And no one knew who he was,
Or how he got past the security door . . .

Or why

Identifying

Of course they wear less hair
            than others,
Keep it tidier—
Everyone knows that.

But even their casual outfits
Are purposeful.

They stand up straighter,
Look beyond your shoulder
When addressing you.

And they call me Sir,
Even though it's obvious
That I work for a living.

I know that the Blue
Will do that to you.

Cash

What Cash lacks in teeth
He makes up for in muscle:
An odd picture always riding
A child's bicycle around town.

Toward me he is ingratiating,
Overly solicitous,
Despite the fact I keep reminding him
I don't have any smokes.

But I do have a package for his woman,
And he insists I go to their apartment
      with it.
He wants me to see how well she is:
"It's good to have her back;
      she looks great!"

She advances through her daughters'
      toys,
Wearing only a faded white blanket
And a shy smile, arm extended,
Lowering slightly her big brown eyes
As she accepts the package.

Cash chats, lingers,
         waits for something.
I turn to go on,
Say goodbye.

Days later I realize
He was pimping her.

In a few weeks she's gone again.
The crime blotter says third offense,
Child/partner abuse.

Cash oversees her three small daughters
Circling the sidewalk like sharks
On pink Barbie bicycles.
"Hey, mailman! Got a smoke?"

Bunny Haven

A decade past high school
She haunts the tidy front porch
Of the otherwise ramshackle old house
Where she lives with her mother
And her particular father.

She thrills to meet the post,
Since I greet her by name each day,
And she warmly pronounces mine.

One day I comment
On an ad addressed
To her and "Bunny Haven."

Yes, she ran a rabbit rescue once,
Right here, in fact,
Until there were too many . . .

She lowers her Irish eyes,
Contains a sigh from long practice.

I suppose the need was endless.

Wild Cat

Like the Looney Tunes cat he
Comes on all spit and slash and sass
(His eyebrows a wild forest),
Emerging from his basement lair
With frayed union suit hems
Peeking out beyond his flannel
       and denims.

The neighborhood legend for his
       birthday binges
On blackberry wine wherever
       they'll still serve him,
His landlord called upon to bail him out
After the ritual brawl and arrest.

Daily he clambers over Buddy
       chained underfoot,
The obese dog yiping
As he's inadvertently kicked.
Buddy's eyes dilate with fear and love.
His Master growls back in reply,
But assures me,
"He won't bite; he's just a pup."
I have it by heart, under my breath.

Each time there follows a litany
        of complaint.
I lean in and listen empathetically.
I promise I'll look into it,
Or I'll return the opened package
        to the Sweepstakes,
Or I just give him a new stamp already.

His blood pressure drops,
He mumbles an apology,
Buddy skulks into the stairway,
And I go in peace.

The Cathedral Portal,
Holy Monday

On the sidewalk here,
A trampled palm frond declares
Royalty passed by.

Duke

Of the Greek nose
And the gunmetal blue eyes
Is ageless.
(Born before they fussed about
        birth certificates, he tells me)

He is a civic landmark
On sixth street,
Opposite the venerable stone church,
More heeded than the speed limit sign,
A patriarch perched above the stream
        of traffic flowing toward the
        Missouri,
Waving in recognition or not
To every third passing pickup truck.

Unchanging as the jokes he retells daily
Is his routine of retrieving
        the neighbor lady's newspaper,
And scuttling to gallantly present it
        through her perpetually sticking
        storm door.

Likewise he's opened the heavy oak
          lobby door of
His century-old brick apartment block
For 23 years of mailmen
(who no longer know there's a key box),
To whom he proudly trumpets that
He never gets a letter anyway.
('Cept that Gospel Mission beggin' for a
          donation!)

As I stuff the antique brass pigeonholes,
He regales me with the full story
Of that drunk Injun
Who collapsed on the sidewalk,
Drawing an aid car,
A long red hook-and-ladder,
And three police cruisers:
A real e-mergency!
He sneers ironically.

Last Christmas, though,
Duke sparkled bright for days
Upon receiving a package:
New jeans, a shirt, and a coat
To warm up the walk to the
          Senior Center.

No, he has no family:
Just a neighbor he had charmed,
Who lived in the mansion cat-a-corner,
A pilot since posted to the Pentagon,
Who has never forgotten
The monument to constancy
Named Duke.

Flyer

The wiry brown girl
Missing two front teeth
Dogs my steps for a block,
Passing behind me
Through every sticking dooryard gate,
Up each paint-peeling porch before
She finally comes to the point.

Did we get mail?
Yes. Your brother took it an hour ago.
What was it?
(I fumble through my bag like an
         amateur magician improvising)
Just this flyer everybody's getting.
From the jail?

I miss a beat.
In my mind's eye I see with her
The commissary birthday card envelope
Bearing a block-printed address
         half remembered,
With a pencil-drawn tattoo rose
You could almost smell
If wishing made things so.

No,
I finally reply:
From GroceryLand.

Oh! I like GroceryLand!

Me too.
I winked—no, winced,
And blinked,
Thinking,
Beats hell outta jail.

Shop Talk

Garrulous Hank just quit talking
After Christmas,
His back twisted from 20 years.
No more Yankee banter
From the bodybuilder
Who cased his mail in just a white
        wife-beater
Before donning the blue shirt
To slide behind the truck wheel
And cruise the cushiest driving route
        in town.

Sergeant Biscuit drawls he'd told him
To take a nice walking route,
Stop reaching from that seat.
He should know,
After 30 years carrying 25 pounds
Nine miles a day
(Plus that extra 30 hanging over
        his wide black belt).
Sarge is still all cuss and fight,
Though he rolls as he walks like a pirate
        on a ship deck.

The doctors stole Jaker's thigh tendon,
Supplanting it in his wrist,
So he could keep on fingering
A couple thousand letters daily,
Flip open mailboxes,
Stuff spring-loaded door slots,
Collate and compress.

But his gait has a hitch now:
Twelve hundred stair steps a day,
Five or six days a week,
Till retirement do us part.

They robbed Peter, yes;
But will Paul be paid?

Inflammation

She sucks cigarettes like a junkie
Shooting up on the sidewalk,
Joyless and determined,
Self-medicating against the pain.

Her hurt is caught by all who watch
Her shuffle down the concrete steps,
Face by now inflamed and red
As her back that never relaxes,
Hands too hot and tingling
From fingering the chain
That holds her together.

She greets me hoarsely,
Wringing courtesy from a moan.
Comfort and camaraderie she finds
Among the weatherworn community
Of butt-enders at the building entry.

They commiserate on patching together
Section Eight and public assistance
To save the cash to buy the drug
That dulls her pain
As it consumes her.

War Song

Shuffling up the sidewalk
To the C-Store
To trade for tobacco,
Grandpa drills the young boy.

Grandpa's proud voice swoops
        and climbs
By turns in chants and whoops
And clicks and moans
Beyond transcribing.

The boy must listen
And assay to mimic,
Only to be reproved,
Improved, for all to hear
As they walk the streets.

His young eyes are hardened,
Steeled by the clash
Of tribal pride
With urban anonymity.
He repeats, none too loudly,
Face toward the pavement,
Unsure where this will lead.

Daisy

When Daisy comes down the sidewalk
On her three-speed,
The little dog on its leash heralds her.
She brightly calls out Hello
In a squeaky cartoonish voice.

Her helmet hides
Her buzz-cut hair:
A sacrifice to compulsion.

If she stops to exchange pleasantries,
I will pause and focus hard
Through her stuttering and facial tics,
Because she's been taught
That engaging the mailman
Is what good neighbors do.

Once she stopped me
To wail and sob
When those bedeviling neighbors
Opened the yard gate
To set her dog loose.

A week later she coos her delight
To be heading to the Biker Church
          Barbeque,
Where a good Lutheran girl
Is set free to raise hands and sway
And speak in tongues
If the Spirit moves.

Dear God,
So much
To transcend.

Exhumed

Refurbishing the garden,
The new homeowners dug up
      Saint Joseph.

Unsure of what to make of his place
      in this deal,
They leaned his undecayed resin form
Against the Craftsman porch pillar's
      pyramidal side,
Between a trowel and an open bag of
      Miracle Grow,
Atop the seven steps I daily climb
      to their mailbox.

Yanked from some dollar-store creche,
Joseph's rapt gaze faces downward,
His arms perpetually outspread,
Palms up,
To indicate the missing Child,
Beckoning me,
In this common place,
To see Him.

Lament

God, this bag is full today!
Eight hundred homes
Of hope and heartache,
And the heavy downfall
Of paper pulp trees,
Leaves noticed by only the lonely.
All fraught with cynicism
Of soldiers whose service
Is recorded merely
As steps per second.

C-Store

The salt of the earth
Can be found downtown
At the seventh street C-Store.

Not in an aisle
But the alley freight door
Where the clerks share a smoke
With customers who have Names.

Whose threadbare tires they fill again,
Volatile tempers they calm,
Diabetic meltdowns they stanch
        with a free candy bar,
Stomach cramps they mop up,
Children they lavishly admire.

It has nothing to do with convenience
And everything to do with community.

Plain Town

In Plain Town
Jazz is a four-letter word,
And hip is the next joint to go
After the knees.

Blacks move along
When they get their orders.
Indian food is frybread, not naan.
And *la lengua no se habla*.
Tacos are hamburger and tater tots.
No Asians here
In this General Motors town.

Every bar doubles down as a Casino.
The Fifties were too good to let go.
Medicare binds us all together,
        indivisible,
        with liberty for just us.
And we are saved by
        the power of Guns.

Foretaste

Flocking like pigeons
At the Cathedral door,
Your poor ones pace,
Awaiting the Friday soup kitchen.

They chatter and strut and preen,
All teasing and smiling.

And when they are full,
Shuffling home with reused
        grocery bags,
The servers disband to the parking lot
And share their own peace there.

Directory

In the corner four-plex
The guy up top has one arm;
The guy below has half one leg.
The guy who puts trash in his mailbox
Wants any extra coupons you have.

Duke at the Salon

On such a mild November 'noon
It did seem about right
To set up shop on
The sixth street sidewalk,
So much better is the light
Than that bare bulb in the basement,
So much easier is the cleanup
With the wind scouring the pavement.

A bath towel is snapped smartly
And coiled about
A neck I recognize.
And I glimpse for the first time
Duke's shining dome
Uncovered by a ballcap,
And wonder that Roger
The codger next door
Can find any hairs there to cut.

Poverty

It stinks
Like stale beer and mold
        in the windowsills.
Tastes like cigarette smoke, not food.
Sounds like screaming
        from the next apartment.
Feels like scouring winter wind drafts
        and endless summer sweat.
Looks like the narrowed eyes
        of distrust born of experience.

School Magnet

In the red-brown-black brick school,
Mostly the mortar is white,
Inhering in its center
To the lively heart of the Office.

Staff circulate their complaints here.
Parents come bearing agendas.
Even the mail must go through
                the front counter.

Those doomed to see the Principal
Agitate while they wait.
Syndromes and spectrums
All come here to roost,
Along with the fallout
Of football on asphalt.

There is much to be learned
About triage and band-aids
And taking your medication,
And who gets free lunch,
And which parent may pick up whom.

In the center,
The highly capable,
Professionally unflappable
Secretary
Manages the flux
Of public education,
And still remembers
How to laugh.

December

Haunting homes alone in the cold dark,
With their blue-lit TVs and
            jabbering News
Beneath the flashing strings of
            icicle lights,
I creep up snow-coated wood steps

And inhale the promise of
            pot roast dinner,
Still two hours and miles away
From my own opened beer
And fingers that will feel.

Cowboy Up

Legless Shane
Does cowboy up
The four-plex basement steps,
Rocking on bare fists,
Pommel and cantle.

Pausing to drag out
His folded wheelchair,
He straightens his thick plastic glasses,
Tips his five-gallon black Stetson,
And smooths his trimmed red mustache

Before wheeling himself
Where he will:
To the Lube Shop,
To chew and spit and rail
As humanity traffics past.

He does not want your sympathy;
Only his autonomy.

CMR's Place

He seized the croup of the mythic West
        as it fled past in rout,
Riding the mangy last bison
Just long enough to look back
        whence it came,
And gather impressions
        for vermilion sunset canvases.

Hard by his Arts and Crafts clapboard
Along the fashionable Avenue,
A log cabin strung of telephone poles
Still heralds the frontier's
        slow-fading romance.

Ice grows thick on the sidewalk
        stamped 1907,
The postman's worn path across
        the brown lawn.
So much changes little here,
Where passage was caught in pigment
To be lamented a little longer.

End Game

The old Cold Warriors debrief daily
Over Senior Coffees at Junior's.
Minds imprinted on Authority
Span global crises in greasy newspapers
Like stiff fingers cradling a lukewarm
        Styrofoam cup.

Time was when they chambered a
        round of H-bomb
In the MAD inverted missile silos
Scarring surrounding wheat fields,
Cocksure despite their mission
Of manning the center of the Soviet
        bull's eye.

The Gym

Some young men love a world of lines:
Red brick hardwood-floored gym,
Concrete steps rising in rank toward
Its doubled doors framed like a goal.

The line you stand in to pay,
And get your clean white towel.
(Better yet: flash a card
To show you belong.)

The painted boundaries marking out
The court on the floor.
Bars on the referee's
Black and white shirt,
As he judges finally
What's in and who's out.

Rows of light bulbs on
The olive drab scoreboard
Instantly reflecting brilliance
And precisely dividing moments.

Lines of latitude
On the rightly spinning auburn globe
As it sinks down the rim.

Lines that define,
Defying transgression.

Yet somehow the color
Remains outside of them.

Misdelivery

Gopher's nephew brakes
His too-small BMX bike,
Dragging his Nikes across the asphalt
Like erasers halting at the curb line.

Waiting for me, he pulls
A rumpled envelope from his jeans
And offers it graciously
If I'll get it to his uncle.

I thank him but stop short
Of dropping it in my satchel:
The jail won't accept postage due
(Nor phone calls: the reason he wrote).

I explain that he can buy a stamp,
If he hurries fast,
Before they roll down
The Post Office's steel curtain.

It's just three blocks:
The old Courthouse.
I smile as I thrust the letter
Back to him.

He thanks me quite politely,
Turns and wheels the other way,
Not willing to play
The fool's game for him.

Valentines

For Valentine's Day
She hit him where it counts·
Kicked her foot right through
His 48-inch TV
And walked away shocked,
Sprinkled with his curses
Like shards of glass,

Only to return moments later
And watch him load once again
His NFL jerseys into his truck,
Witnessed by his parents,
Who had rolled up in their Buick,
And from a distance by a cop,
Also called,
Who parked in the alley
And ate a sandwich.

This is the drama they replay
On Saturdays,
From the heart.

Lunch Break, Wednesday

I come here to kneel
At his feet,
To feel
His filthy thumb
Abruptly swipe the flesh
Of my wrinkled brow
With that remarkable
Sign of violence.

Breath seizes in my throat
At the primal words
Of truth
That rock my core
Since Adam:

"Remember that you are dust,
And to dust you shall return."

I whisper Amen.

The Ritz

Jensen's place has gone all to hell
Ever since Mrs. Severe Bob
Got fed up and left.

She used to scrub the ninety-year old
        marble steps,
The mosaic tile lobby floor.
The endless fir stairs smelled
        of Murphy's Wood Soap
Through all their elegantly tall
        four storeys.

But the Old Man just taped off
The broken-down antique cage elevator
And turned the grounds into
A perpetual garage sale.

He let the dogs in, too, in pairs,
To fill the void left in his chest,
To water her planted roses
And bark when the cops show up
Looking for the Fence.

A good woman makes all the difference.

Pensioner

Most days he walks across my route,
Avoiding eye contact,
Though I am his mailman,
And I wave.

A dingy tan overcoat
Reveals a few inches of jeans
And black sneakers.

He skirts the Donut Shop
But never stops there
On his way to the park
With the tall swing set.

On it he pumps like an eight-year old,
Pointing toes to the heavens,
Face as unfathomable
As his photo grey lenses,

But straining muscles rocking
To an inner rhythm
Undeniable,
All his own.

84

Annunciation Day

Driving away from Express delivery
By overnight mail from Kalamazoo,
Marked "HUMAN REMAINS,"
(But far too light to be complete--
      or to be adult . . .)

I'm stopped by the Importunate Woman
      from Thirteenth Street,
Flashing her monocle headlight,
Cursing casually,
Again after her old man's
      unemployment check.

"I'm bleeding all over the place
      or I'd get out.
Sorry to bother you, but I need pads.
He left without leaving me money.
It's my period. Thank you."

While rifling her 3 pm post at 9 am,
I tell her I'm sorry too . . .
For the loss of her neighbor and friend
Run over crossing Fourteenth Street.

She touches my arm.
"Thank you.
Took her clear out of her shoes.
I went to the wake yesterday — real sad.
She'd slept on my couch
        just the night before,
When the Old Guy she takes care of
Had his sister come stay."

The next night she lay on the pavement.

I wondered as I left the Funeral Home
        parking lot,
If yesterday she had rested
On a velveteen casket liner,
Or if her ashes were boxed to go —
And where?

When the world is overturned,
Blessed are those nearest abasement.

Today I Have Been Instructed

That I am not to put my hands
        in my pockets
While walking in the cold,
As it is unsafe.
(Perhaps I need to buy better gloves?)

That I must not forget things.

That I should walk consistently
        120 steps per minute
While accurately collating letters
        with my hands
And balancing random-sized mail
In the crook of my (left) arm.

That I have been witnessed stomping
        on porch steps.
(Perhaps to count them?
Perhaps to break them?)

Such practices are not efficient
        nowadays
"In our competitive situation where
Everything is micro-managed."

It is suggested that
Perhaps I would like to be inspected
For five consecutive days?

It is desired that I comply
Until such time as I retire
[a consummation devoutly
        to be wished].

Funny Business

Like the Ghosts of Trust Long Past,
The Funeral Directors
Still wear dark suit vests
And brandish pocket watches,
Synchronized with the American Legion
        Rifle Squad.

More than just embalmers,
Now that incineration has taken off,
They are Packagers of Life Stories,
Dealing in satellite radio nostalgic music
And family snapshot slide shows
        on Power Point,
Artisanal collectible urns,
And moving trifold display boards
        of mementoes.

Death is thriving here and now,
Where the Harley riders' cortege is
Drowning out the Undertaker's voice,
And the pink Shriners' clown car at the
Ivied brick mortuary Welcome sign
Eludes the notice of Management,
But beckons my cellphone camera.

Pawn

His paper route finished early,
Doug's first in line
At the hock shop
Twelve minutes before opening.

A toaster and three DVD's
Tucked under his shivering arm,
Eight days yet
Till the first of the month.

I try to avoid looking at him,
But he calls out to me,
His friend,
His Paperboy.

Managed Care

Legless Eileen,
Queen of the sidewalk smokers' klatch,
Is so delighted "the Cute Mailman"
Is back in shorts now.
(Accenting his varicose veins)

I think she's glad to be back herself,
Disrupted from her children's farm
When she missed too much
This crumbling old folks' home,
The last stop before Hospice.

Here she can watch boys along the Ave
From her wheelchair's folding throne.
She can rustle up microwave popcorn
            in the Visitors' Lounge,
And chime in her truth at Bible Study.

She wears unfazed the purple welts
Across her cheek and brow
From when the oxygen exploded
As she lit up another scrounged butt.

That bandaged eye was bum already
From diabetes anyway.
And what's left to live for
Any more
If not the simple pleasures
Of holding court
And lighting up,
Sassy.

Hit and Run

Like an oily iodine,
Red pepper spray
Stings and stains,
Blending with blood
From my tooth-punched hand
That held the punctured can
In the Rottweiler's face.

The owners vanish cursing,
The dog bolts squealing away.
I wrap up in my handkerchief
And head for band-aids
From my lunchbox.

I guess it had learned to hate blue.

Poor Tax

He drops his borrowed bicycle
At the Courthouse back door,
Beneath the green copper dome
Topped by Lady Just Us'
Broad white ass.
Her blindfold assures
No eye contact will be made.
Her scale pans are held up
For more coin.

It is time
To spend a night in jail,
In lieu of the grand
That could in theory buy
Required liability insurance
For the $300 beater
Whose busted headlight
Landed him a court date
For DWI—
Driving While Indian.

Duke Across Town

Has the lone wolf of Sixth Street
Been tamed by free teatime ice cream
At the nursing home where he landed
When a nice woe-man friend
Started checking on his health?

Oh, he still keeps his distance
From them rich widders
Retired across the Avenue.
But he can't shake Arthur Itis
Dogging his steps.

And he still postures, ribs,
And gossips in stage whispers,
Holding your eye with steely stare.

But there is no traffic here,
Save wheelchairs piloted by veterans
Of the pancreatic wars.

Walking bandy-legged
        as an old cowboy,
He seems reassured
That there still are Injuns about.

However, I see that
He must have let some young
        Nurse's Aide
Pluck that lone defiant hair
That sprouted from the middle
Of his proud strong nose.

I guess it was time.

Holed Up

Dred went and did it.
Two months unemployed,
High again,
He walked across the street
To the bank—
His bank—
And held it up with a gun
For eight hundred bucks.

Tall and black with wild hair
And wilder dilated eyes,
He innocuously returned,
Waiting for the crossing light,
His backpack harboring
        the gun and the cash.

Then he turned a block north
        to the C-Store,
Bought a money order to pay
        past due rent,
A few smokes, a six-pack;
And returned two blocks to home—
Suddenly surrounded by the K-9 Unit
And a flashing light show.

The Chopper came next,
Buzzing the neighborhood
While my boss walked behind me
Holding a clipboard.

"Bet they're looking for one of my
                customers,"
I smirked,
Just going with the odds.

That night I heard it on the news:
They found him crouched in the bushes
Beside the apartment door.

The next day the breakroom buzz
Was that I had been right
Alright.

Too bad Dred was wrong
In his poor exchange,
Losing so much more than his lease.

Tips

In a square white plastic box
        behind the truck seat,
Brimming with red and green
        curling ribbon
And silver-white-gold envelopes
        unstamped,
I keep the holiday tips I gather
        in December:

Candy of all sorts and always
Dollar Store Chocolate Cherry Cordials,
Gift cards for lunch at Dairy Queen,
Cookies for calories I burn through
        (sometimes for dogs to toss to),
And fives or tens or even twenties
        (though a penny over my limit).

Then there are cocoa and coffee and tea,
        though packaged dry and cold,
And Jesus Loves You resin figurines
        with large and poignant eyes,
And chemical handwarmers,
And a plush acrylic sweater,
And bottles of wine brought to the curb.

But the one I hold on to is my
        birthstone,
From Virginia who first bawled
When I replaced her favorite mailman.

Later she'd wait daily to chat me up,
Until the pancreatic cancer.
Then she solemnly placed my hand
      on her belly
To verify that she had no more time left
To fashion a ring for this,
And so must leave it to me.

Merry Christmas!

She was gone before February.

Losing

Word is: Martin's losing it.
He's still got the walrus mustache,
Yeah;
And the hot red nylon stocking cap too.
But the twinkling eyes,
The snaggle-toothed smile?
Sometimes they're a no-show.

Fact is: He didn't show up at
        TastiFreeze
For three whole days.
The Assistant Manager finally
        walked across the street,
Found his hidden apartment door,
And rousted him from bed,
Like he was staff and not a customer.
He "forgot to wake up."

Forgot?
The man parlayed a dollar cup of joe
Into a place at the City Gate;
A fixture more dependable than
        that soda dispenser;

Puts in more hours here than
        the Shift Boss.
If Martin goes,
Who will regale my lunch table
With stories of how it was when,
Or those same tired old jokes?
Who will wash dinner dishes
        at the Moose Lodge?
Who will use those Walmart gift cards
        I tuck quietly under his door?

Oh, I know
He's been in his 80's forever,
Got more wrinkles than God;
Only now he's forgetting . . .

Forgetting to wear socks,
Forgetting where he lives,
Forgetting to look before crossing.

We'll all lose then.

Parting

When my working days are yester-
I'll wear no more polyester.

About the Author

Rob Wilson studied English at the University of Washington before serving in the Air Force and the Postal Service in Washington and Montana. He is retired, with his wife Gretchen, and enjoys being with his grandchildren, keeping a few animals, reading, volunteering in the community, and— still—walking outdoors.

www.ingramcontent.com/pod-product-compliance
Lightning Source LLC
Chambersburg PA
CBHW021129020426
42331CB00005B/688